Communication

Powerful Ways Explode Your Business by Increasing your Reach with Modern Communication (Networking, Social Media, Customers, etc)

Robert S. Parker

Contents

Introduction 9

Chapter 1. Why You Need To Build A Powerful Business Network 15

Chapter 2. Ask Customers For Referrals 22

Chapter 3. Use Testimonials 29

Chapter 4. Participate In Industry Conferences 36

Chapter 5. Blog Regularly 43

Chapter 6. Use Social Media 50

Chapter 7. How To Be Visible 57

Chapter 8. How To Make An Impact 64

Chapter 9. How To Engage Effectively 72

Chapter 10. Be Ready To Face Rejection 79

Chapter 11. Build Trust and Relationships 85

© Copyright 2019 by Robert S. Parker- All rights reserved.

This document is geared toward providing exact and reliable information in regard to the topic and issue covered. The publication is sold with the idea that the publisher is not required to render accounting, officially permitted, or otherwise, qualified services. If advice is necessary, legal or professional, a practiced individual in the profession should be ordered.

- From a Declaration of Principles which was accepted and approved equally by a Committee of the American Bar Association and a Committee of Publishers and Associations.

In no way is it legal to reproduce, duplicate, or transmit any part of this document in either electronic means or in printed format. Recording of this publication is strictly prohibited and any storage of this document is not allowed unless with written permission from the publisher. All rights reserved.

The information provided herein is stated to be truthful and consistent, in that any liability, in terms of inattention or otherwise, by any usage or abuse of any policies, processes, or directions contained within is the solitary and utter responsibility of the recipient reader. Under no circumstances will any legal responsibility or blame be held against the publisher for any reparation, damages, or monetary loss due to the information herein, either directly or indirectly.

Respective authors own all copyrights not held by the publisher.

The information herein is offered for informational purposes solely, and is universal as so. The presentation of the information is without contract or any type of guarantee assurance.

The trademarks that are used are without any consent, and the publication of the trademark is without permission or backing by the trademark owner. All trademarks and brands within this book are for clarifying purposes only and are the owned by the owners themselves, not affiliated with this document.

Introduction

A powerful business network is the single most important factor that can help you to grow your business. Successful entrepreneurs are adept at building powerful business networks. They use several proven steps that enable them to reach out and connect with potential clients.

Having friends from different fields and locations can help you to get the support you need to survive in a volatile and unpredictable business environment. You need to create a strategy plan to convey your message to your target audience. Make plans for the long term and keep in touch with your network regularly. Remember to follow up on promises others make to you as well as promises you make to others.

It takes time to build strong relationships and as an entrepreneur you need to know about the tools that can help you to establish your own network quickly. Your existing customers can help you to build your credibility and reputation. You need to ask your customers for referrals and testimonials while you are working with them. Think of it as searching for opportunities to help people rather than as hard selling.

You need to take part in industry meetings because face-to-face communication can help you to build rapport. Take opportunities to speak at public events and write authoritative articles for industry publications.

Be prepared to tell people about what you do and how your products or services are superior to those offered by your competitors. Learn the art of chatting with people and look for common interests so you can have a mutually rewarding conversation. This will help you to find reasons to meet again in the future.

The words of Joyce Meyer help us to appreciate the importance of being positive in our interactions:

"We can improve our relationships with others by leaps and bounds if we become encouragers instead of critics."

Joyce Meyer

Social media is a powerful tool that no business can afford to ignore. Take time to understand the differences between the most popular social media platforms and focus on the ones that are suitable for you. Post engaging content regularly to build a loyal fan following.

Blogging can help you to share your knowledge and experience with people from across the world. It adds fresh, relevant content to your website, which attracts potential customers and is good for search engine optimization (SEO).

To expand your business network, you need to be visible and make an impact. Take on positions of leadership whenever you get the opportunity. Identify your target audience and look for ways to connect and engage with them.

Be prepared to face criticism, opposition and rejection when you become successful and take on positions of leadership. Think of criticism as something that is rooted in the insecurity of others and take it in your stride. Have big dreams and focus on achieving them instead of thinking about your critics.

Look for ways to build strong relationships and trust with the members of your business network. Be ready to help people without thinking of what you will get in return. Focus on growing and renewing your network continuously as some members will inevitably move on. Remember that a powerful business network is your most valuable asset!

Chapter 1. Why You Need To Build A Powerful Business Network

A powerful business network is crucial for success because people prefer to do business with those they like and trust. Business decisions are made by people not companies, and people prefer to depend on those who they know will deliver what they need at the right time. The survival and growth of a business can depend on the strength of its business network.

Once people have worked with you for a while, they will start trusting you. They will know that you do what you say and that in turn will help them to meet targets or commitments they have made to their employers or customers. If people know that you stick to your commitments and deliver on time, they will be happy to recommend you to their friends.

To grow your business and prosper, you need to have a proven track record. You need to build your reputation as someone who can deliver quality products or services on time. A good reputation will help you to establish a powerful network of happy customers who are willing to provide testimonials, referrals, and advice. Your network will make it much easier for you to take your business to the next level.

Brian Koslow's words show how a good reputation can be the best advertisement:

"There is no advertisement as powerful as a positive reputation traveling fast."

Brian Koslow

Once you are known as the best person to go to for the goods or services you offer, you will have all the customers and orders you can handle. You will not have to struggle to find new customers and can choose to work with regular customers who provide larger orders with higher margins. You will have more time to focus on improving performance and customer satisfaction.

A powerful business network can be your most valuable asset. It can provide a wider moat that will protect your business from the competition, especially in adverse market conditions. You will have a bigger competitive edge if you offer something that no one else has and deliver more than the customer expects. Your regular customers will think of you as a valued partner because your products or services will help them to succeed and prosper.

Once you have built a strong business network, you can get support and advice from industry experts whenever you need it. You will not have to make decisions based on limited information, which can lead to costly mistakes. All you need to do when you need guidance is to pick up the phone and talk to someone who knows more than you about the issues you are concerned about. Better business decisions will help you to expand and become more profitable!

If you offer excellent products or services, you will be known as an expert and more and more people will seek your advice. This can provide great opportunities for you to reach out to those you don't know. While you may feel that this is taking up a lot of your time and you are not getting anything in return, remember that it will help you to expand your network.

A powerful business network can help you to scale up your business rapidly. Once you are confident about your ability to meet the specific requirements of your target market and are getting more orders than you can handle, you can scale up and diversify. Your business network will push you to expand capacity because the success of your customers depends on your ability to meet their growing requirements.

Your network can provide different types of support to help you to achieve the success you have been dreaming of. Those who think of you as a partner will go out of their way to provide the support you need to grow your business. They may offer business and technical guidance and some may even offer financial help to enable you to boost capacity.

A strong business network can be the single most important factor on which your success depends. If building a powerful business network is so important to your success, can you really afford to neglect it? You need to create a strategy to build strong relationships with those who can be crucial for your success.

If you have been getting limited success for a while, you may find that you have not been putting much time and effort into building and nourishing your business network. If you want to turn your dreams into reality, focus on building a powerful business network. You need to take action now to harness the power of your business network!

These questions will help you to take the right steps to build a powerful business network:

1. Name the factors that give your business a unique competitive edge.
2. Name your most important customers
3. Do you keep in touch with all your customers regularly?
4. What steps can you take to expand your business network?

Chapter 2. Ask Customers For Referrals

The easiest way to expand your business network is to ask your customers for referrals while you are working with them. Customers who trust you and are satisfied with your products or services will be happy to provide referrals. They will know people in the industry who are also searching for products or services like yours. Being referred by someone who has worked with you makes it much easier for you to expand your business network and get more customers.

W. Edwards Deming's words highlight the important role your customers can play in helping you to expand your business:

"Profit in business comes from repeat customers, customers that boast about your project or service, and that bring friends with them."

W. Edwards Deming

It is best to ask customers for referrals while you are working closely with them and providing outstanding service. There is no need to be hesitant about asking for referrals or to postpone it until the work is completed. If you leave it too late, it may never get done.

Bear in mind that asking for referrals is not hard selling. You are in the business of providing outstanding products or services to your customers. Asking for referrals is in fact seeking opportunities to provide the same outstanding products or services to others. You need to make it a standard part of your communication with your customers. Referrals from satisfied customers can add thousands of dollars to your bottom line.

You need to assume that your customers will be happy to refer you. If you get the sense that they are uncomfortable about referring you to their friends, ask them about the reasons for this. You may find that they are not fully satisfied with some aspects of your products or services. This can provide valuable insights that will help you to improve customer satisfaction.

If you find that some customers are unhappy with your products or services, analyze the reasons for this. There may be areas in which you don't possess a strong competitive edge. In this case, you can try to improve your products or services or consider exiting these areas so you can focus on doing what you do best. In either case, asking for referrals will help to improve your business prospects.

It is best to keep in touch with your current and past customers regularly. Ask them how they are doing and tell them about how important their referrals are to your success. They will be happy to help you if you communicate with them regularly and appreciate their contribution to your success.

Make it very easy for your customers to refer you to their colleagues and friends. People who want to refer you to their friends may not know how to clearly communicate what you are good at. You can make it easier for your customers to refer you by clearly communicating what you do and why your customers prefer to deal with you. This information can be listed in your brochures, newsletters, and other communications along with your contact details. The back of your business card can also include a request for referrals.

Remember to thank customers who provide referrals. You may want to call or email them to express your gratitude. You also need to provide referrals to your customers. Helping people regardless of whether you get something in return or not can provide unexpected rewards. A small gift can also help you to express your gratitude to those who referred you. The value of the gift can depend on the number of referrals or business volume generated.

Business networking groups ask their members to inform and educate each other about their businesses, products and services. These groups meet at regular intervals and remind members to generate referrals for each other. This forces business owners to think about how they can use referrals to generate business for themselves and each other on a day-to-day basis.

Provide clear instructions about how your customers can post reviews of your products or services on professional websites. All your communications, including your newsletters, emails, and social media business profiles, need to include links to review websites that feature you. Your website also needs to include links that direct people to such reviews.

It is easy to generate business through referrals. All you need to do is to develop the habit of asking every customer to help you by providing a few referrals. It will not cost anything and it can help you to add thousands of dollars to your bottom line. Even if a customer is reluctant to provide referrals, it will help you identify causes of dissatisfaction. So go ahead and leverage the power of your network to expand your business!

These questions will help you to focus on getting more referrals from your existing customers:

1. Do you ask all your customers for referrals?
2. Do you thank customers for referrals?
3. Do you reward customers who offer the most referrals?
4. Do you think that asking for referrals is hard selling?

Chapter 3. Use Testimonials

Testimonials provided by happy customers can be a powerful tool that convinces people to try out your products or services. Potential customers are more likely to be convinced by the unbiased recommendations of your existing customers than a sales pitch that lists the features and benefits of your products or services. Rave reviews prove that you have been providing very high levels of customer satisfaction consistently.

People are bombarded by so many offers for similar products and services that it is very hard for them to decide about what to buy. They are confused by the flood of offers and tend to get paralyzed due to information overload. In such a situation, testimonials can help potential customers to make up their minds about which offer is right for them.

Your testimonials are a valuable asset that can help you to overcome skepticism and convince potential customers to try out your products or services. Brian Tracy's words help us to appreciate the importance of making the most of testimonials:

"Your company's most valuable asset is how it is known to its customers."

Brian Tracy

If your customers can't stop talking about what a great experience you gave them, you will not have to work too hard to sell yourself. That's why the most successful business people are willing to go the extra mile to make all of their customers very happy. Positive reviews from happy customers build their reputation and make it easy for them to get all the leads, customers and orders they can handle.

Testimonials are much more convincing because they are written in the voice of the customer. They convey what the customer liked most about your products or services. Testimonials are different from your sales pitch because people can see that they are a frank and impartial account of what your customers experienced while using your products or services.

Testimonials prove to people that your customers are willing to tell others about what a great experience you gave them. This shows that your customers trust you enough to take the risk of recommending you to others. People who read testimonials posted on your website will realize that you are an experienced professional with a proven track record.

You can post testimonials in different forms, on your online profile and website. Text, audio or video testimonials can be a powerful persuasive component of your website. They can help to convert many visitors into customers. People who visit your website can see what your customers actually experienced when they used your products or services. If you provided measurable benefits, you can ask your customers to communicate this with facts and figures.

Pick testimonials that provide details of key benefits offered by your products or services. A general testimonial that says you are great and your products are wonderful may not be as effective as one that mentions tangible benefits in terms of higher sales or profits, lower costs or time saved. Testimonials that mention how your products or services helped customers to solve specific problems are more persuasive. Prominently display testimonials provided by people with whom your potential customers can identify.

Your testimonials need to back the claims that you make about your products or services. They need to focus on the key factors that make your offerings better than those of your competitors. Comparative statements made by your customers about how they tried other products and services that did not work before they found out about you can help to convince potential customers.

If you have been in business for a while, you will probably have a large number of testimonials from satisfied clients. However, if you are starting out in business or if you have still not received many testimonials, you need to ask your customers for them. You could add a link or auto responder to your website that requests customers to provide feedback.

If you have launched your business recently and have no testimonials, you could request a few people to try out your products or services for free and ask them to provide feedback. Ask customers if you can use their testimonials on your website and post the best ones prominently on the top, center and side bars of your website's home page. Positive reviews need to be displayed throughout your website and you also need to have a dedicated testimonials page.

Remember that making up testimonials or using testimonials without permission does not pay. Readers can detect fake testimonials and it can make them suspect everything else you tell them. Use customer testimonials as they are, without any editing or proofreading. This makes them more credible and visitors are more likely to feel that they are genuine and unbiased. Start using the power of positive testimonials to grow your business now!

These questions will help you to focus on how you can make the best use of testimonials:

1. Are you using testimonials to generate business?
2. Are your customers happy to provide good testimonials?
3. Does your website display your best testimonials prominently?
4. What steps can you take to get more testimonials?

Chapter 4. Participate In Industry Conferences

You need to participate in industry conferences to build your business network quickly. You may feel that you can access all the information you need via the Internet and there is no need to take time out from your busy schedule to attend industry conferences. While it is true you can find a huge amount of relevant information online, this is not a substitute for having face-to-face meetings with experienced industry professionals.

Raymond Arroyo's words help us to appreciate the importance of meeting people face-to-face to build rapport and trust:

"Many believe effective networking is done face-to-face, building a rapport with someone by looking at them in the eye, leading to a solid connection and foundational trust."

Raymond Arroyo

You can get valuable information and advice by chatting with people informally at industry events. Innovative ideas and concepts provided by experienced professionals can help you to transform your business. Searching for information online cannot provide as much value because you may not even be aware of the latest trends and innovations which can make a huge difference to your business and life.

These industry events are a great place to connect and build strong relationships with people who are dealing with similar issues. This includes potential customers, suppliers, vendors, and competitors. People from different locations and markets can share valuable insights and advice with you. This can help you to learn about how you can leverage your strengths, enhance customer satisfaction and improve your competitive edge.

Many business people are reluctant to talk to competitors. They fear that their competitors may find out too much about how they work and may even walk away with their customers. If you are wary of interacting with your competitors, bear in mind that collaboration can help you to learn, improve and grow faster. Working in isolation is likely to limit your success. If you share your experiences, you will be able to learn a lot of new things that will help you to improve performance and make more money.

Those you help will remember you and will become supportive members of your business network. You can look forward to meeting them at other industry events. People from other areas can provide referrals and advice on best practices. You can learn a lot from them and can also provide referrals and guidance to them. You need to have as many friends as you can from different areas if you want to grow your business quickly. A supportive business network can be a huge help when you are struggling to solve difficult problems in adverse market conditions.

Industry conferences can help you to position yourself as an expert in your field by speaking at public events and writing authoritative articles for industry publications. Articles published in industry publications may be read by thousands of people from across the world. You can include your contact details and links that lead to your other articles, profiles and website. Being known as an expert in your field will make it much easier for you to grow your business.

Exhibitions that are organized at industry events provide a great opportunity to see what vendors and suppliers have to offer. You can talk to sales people and learn about the latest developments in your field. Vendors and suppliers can provide details of innovative products and services that will help you improve your competitive edge. They can help you to understand emerging industry trends and suggest ways of preparing your business for imminent changes in the business environment.

Industry events allow you to study your competitors and to find out how they operate. You can study how they meet the specific needs of their customers and compare their business models with your own. You can identify specific market segments in which you have a significant competitive advantage and focus your time energy and resources on meeting their needs. These ideas and insights can be the real reward that you get by taking time to attend industry events.

Industry conferences also offer great opportunities to relax. Most business people get very little time to rest and have a good time. They are so stressed out that they are not able to see the big picture or to make plans for the future. You can plan short vacations when you travel to attend industry events. This can help you to get much needed rest and to plan for the future.

Industry events force us to take time off from our busy schedules to interact with other professionals who are facing the problems and issues that we struggle to solve every day. Before you give the next industry conference a pass, think about what you could be missing out on. Industry conferences can help you to change the course of your business and your life!

These questions will help you to use industry conferences to develop your business network:

1. Do you know about the industry conferences that are relevant to you?
2. Do you speak in public at industry conferences?
3. Do you write articles for industry publications?
4. Do you share information and advice with people from your industry?

Chapter 5. Blog Regularly

Posting relevant, engaging blog content regularly will help you to grow your business network. Blogging can enable you to share your knowledge and experience with others. Potential customers and others who are interested in your field will appreciate the value of your blog posts. They will visit your website regularly, sign up for your newsletter and want to read any book you publish.

The words of Paulo Coelho help us to appreciate the value of sharing our thoughts, ideas and opinions with others:

"Writing means sharing. It's part of the human condition to want to share things - thoughts, ideas, opinions."

Paulo Coelho

Your blog can help you to establish yourself as an expert in your field. It can build credibility and trust with potential customers. You will gain respect and people will think of you as an experienced professional. You may be invited to write articles and speak at conferences as an industry expert. This will make it much easier for you to expand your network and your business.

Publishing long blog posts frequently can help your website to get higher search engine rankings, and this will result in increased traffic. More people will sign up for your newsletter and your business network will grow. You will get many more leads, customers, and orders.

Long posts could mean more than 500 words and frequent posting could mean several times a day, week or month, depending on how much time you can spare. You can decide on the length and frequency of your posts based on your own convenience, but it is best to post at least once a week.

You can boost website traffic organically by posting good content on your blog regularly. You can also use paid advertisements, which will bring potential customers to your website. Your advertisements will be displayed whenever people enter the keywords you have specified in the search engines. You can consider using paid advertisements to boost website traffic quickly. Try out different keywords, advertisements, locational targeting, etc. until you get the desired results.

Once your blog starts attracting a lot of traffic, you can consider displaying advertisements on your website. You will get a small amount every time a visitor clicks on an advertisement displayed on your website. This can generate a small income, which will help you to recover some or all of the money you have invested in your website. However, this would only be worthwhile if your website is getting a large number of unique visitors every month.

Set aside some time every month to write your blog posts. You can write blog posts for several weeks whenever you have time to spare. Once you have written posts for a few weeks, you need to check, edit and polish them several times to ensure that they will make an impact on readers. You can create a schedule according to which the posts will be published automatically on dates you have specified in advance. This will help to ensure that your website will always have fresh content, which keeps visitors engaged and is good for SEO.

There is no need to only publish long blog posts that involve a lot of in-depth research. You can create shorter posts based on your existing brochures or sales flyers as well as accounts of what you experienced while you were travelling.

Interesting photos you have taken yourself or those purchased from websites that offer stock photos for as little as a dollar apiece can add a lot of value to your blog posts. Relevant pictures that have not been published elsewhere can improve your website's search engine rankings.

Maintain a scrapbook to collect any ideas you may get while you are doing other work. This could be in the form of relevant studies, stories, pictures, quotations, etc. This material can help you to create blog posts in the future. It is much easier to write articles when you are constantly searching for interesting news and ideas. Your scrapbook will help to ensure that you will not face writer's block when you sit down to write.

If you don't like to write or if you don't have the time to create your own blog posts, you can ask someone else to do it for you. You could ask members of your staff, freelance writers, writing services or others to create content for your blog. You can edit the posts to ensure that they are in your voice and are in line with what you want to say.

As more and more people visit your blog and sign up for your newsletter, your business network will grow and you will be able to take your business to the next level. So act now and start posting relevant content regularly on your blog!

These questions will help you to use your blog to expand your business network:

1. How many people follow your blog?
2. Do people participate and comment on your blog posts?
3. Are you posting engaging blog content regularly?
4. Do you need to outsource content creation for your blog?

Chapter 6. Use Social Media

Social media is a powerful tool that can help you to expand your business network quickly. It can enable you to reach out and engage thousands of people from across the world who may be interested in your products or services. Once you have understood the differences between the various social media websites, you can start using some of them as part of your overall business networking strategy.

Social media has become an essential tool for all those who are trying to connect with potential customers. It is even more important if you sell services because it allows potential customers to find out all they need to know about you before they contact you. Service-focused businesses that are transparent and willing to share more information about what they are good at are likely to attract more customers.

The words of Carol Roth help us to appreciate the importance of using social media to reach out to customers:

"Social media can be a powerful tool to listen to, engage with and gain access to customers that you would otherwise not be able to connect with."

Carol Roth

Each social media platform is suitable for different types of requirements. For example, LinkedIn and Google+ are more suitable for professional communications. Snapchat and Twitter specialize in brief, quick communications. Pinterest and Instagram are suitable for posting images. Facebook is a very versatile platform that you can use after you have set up your own website and blog.

You need to identify which social media networks your potential customers use. Once you have come up with a list of social media websites, you can pick the most popular one to start with. Don't try to do too much initially because you may not have enough time to create and post a lot of high-quality content frequently. Start with one social media website and build up your profile and content on it. Once you have a following on one social media website, you can consider posting on others.

If you identify customer needs that are currently not being met, you can tailor your content to fill these gaps. You can create posts that will meet the needs of your potential customers depending on the products and services you would like to promote. Your content needs to be aimed at informing and educating consumers and building trust. If you create posts aimed mainly at selling, you may get limited success in social media.

Posting a large amount of content or attracting hundreds of followers need not be your main goal. Aim to connect and engage with potential customers and inform them about your products or services. In general, the posts across social media websites that get the best response tend to be the ones that have lots of images and videos providing step-by-step instructions on how to solve problems.

You can create posts about exciting new products and the latest deals that you are offering. It is essential to respond to comments and questions posted by followers in a casual and fun way. Your blog posts can include tips on how to make the best possible use of your products or services. Tips on how to maintain and repair products will also be appreciated by your followers.

Trial and error will help you to discover what your follower's value most. While it is best to focus on giving them what you know they want, you can keep experimenting with new types of content to keep everything fresh, interesting and exciting for your regulars. You need to make a social media plan that spells out who you are targeting, the type of content and your posting calendar. Be clear about what you will post and when.

It takes time to attract a significant number of followers, so be patient. While you may want to create a sensational post that will go viral and help you to attract thousands of followers overnight, in reality this is highly unlikely. You need to have the right mindset and put a lot time and effort into building a dedicated fan base on social media.

Social media can help you to display your brand to thousands of potential customers from across the world, and you can do this at no cost or a very small cost. Engaging content can increase brand recall because it will be posted in so many places. It will also help you to get better search engine rankings.

Social media can help you to find out about customer dissatisfaction before it becomes a major problem. Take the first step and start using the power of social networking to expand your business network now!

These questions will help you to harness the power of social media to grow your business network:

1. Do you actively use social media to engage with customers?
2. Do you have a social media plan and do you follow it?
3. Do you inform and educate customers instead of selling to them?
4. Do you respond promptly to negative feedback posted on social media?

Chapter 7. How To Be Visible

You can grow your business network quickly by being visible in your community and industry. Consider joining your local chamber of commerce and industry associations that are relevant to your business. Attend industry conferences and be prepared to deliver an elevator pitch that summarizes what you do and why your customers prefer to deal with you.

Take time to learn about how you can raise the visibility of your business. Create a plan and decide about what you can to do to make your business more visible. If you are not inclined to make a plan or feel you can't do it yourself, consider speaking to a public relations consultant who will help you to identify your goals, your target audiences, key messages, and the best methods you can use to increase the visibility of your business.

Be forthright and speak frankly at meetings and conferences whenever you feel you have something to contribute. Accept offers to speak at public events related to your community and industry. Your contributions will be welcomed and people will consider you to be an authority in your field. You will start getting more and more invitations to speak at public events. This will also help you to develop your skills and confidence as a public speaker.

Public speaking can make it much easier for you to increase visibility and expand your business network. The words of Lowell Thomas help us to appreciate the importance of developing the ability to speak in public:

"The ability to speak is a short cut to distinction. It puts a man in the limelight, raises him head and shoulders above the crowd."

Lowell Thomas

Write articles in local newspapers and industry publications related to your field. Be ready to do interviews with local newspapers whenever you get the opportunity. Once you are known as an expert in your field, more and more opportunities of this type will come your way. You need to be prepared and keep a professional digital picture ready for such occasions.

Step forward and be ready to take on positions of leadership whenever you are asked to do so. Many business people feel that they are too busy to spend time on such activities. The truth is that taking up leadership positions can help you to gain respect and grow your business much faster. It will provide a huge boost to your reputation and credibility and do wonders for your business network.

A professionally designed website with compelling content will help you to increase visibility. You need to clearly identify your target customers and create content that is specifically targeted at them. Include relevant keywords in your page titles and content. This will help to improve your website's search engine rankings.

Make your website more visible by sharing links on a reciprocal basis with companies and organizations that have complementary businesses. Include the link of your website in all your communications, including your emails, newsletters, product literature, letterhead, visiting cards, company van, etc.

If you have any news that could interest potential customers, you can create and distribute press releases about it. If you don't know how to do this or don't have the time to do it yourself, you can ask a professional press release writing service or freelancer to write and distribute press releases for you. This will help to increase awareness about who you are and what you do. Press releases include your profile, contact details and a link to your website to make it easy for people to reach you.

You can distribute a newsletter at regular intervals to keep members of your network engaged. Asking people who visit your website to sign up for your newsletter is a great way of expanding your business network. You can offer visitors a free eBook that provides valuable information and advice. Providing useful information and advice to potential customers will encourage them to join your business network and remain in it.

Volunteering can help you to contribute to the greater good and it will also help you to expand your business network. Search for volunteering opportunities in your area which are in line with your interests and values. Be willing to sponsor community projects and take on leadership roles if the opportunity arises. Your expertise and skills may be greatly valued by community organizations.

Use social media to become more visible and engage with potential customers. An effective social media campaign can help you to grow your business network quickly. Take time to learn about the different social media websites. Add a blog to your website to share your knowledge and experience with others. Act now to increase your visibility and grow your business network!

These questions will help you to find effective ways of making yourself more visible:

1. Have you identified your target audiences?
2. What messages do you want to convey to them?
3. How can you reach out connect with them?
4. Are there any leadership positions that you can take on?

Chapter 8. How To Make An Impact

To succeed and make an impact in business networking, you need to be clear about your goals and the steps that will help you to achieve them. It is essential to remember that business networking is not about selling your products or services. To be a successful networker, try to engage and help people. Show genuine interest in others and try to build trust and relationships. You will not be successful if you focus only on what you can get out of interactions.

If you are genuinely interested in helping others regardless of whether you get anything in return or not, people will like you and want to connect with you. On the other hand, if you are only interested in selling your products or services, they will quickly realize that you don't care about them. This can make a huge difference to the way people react to you and how successful you will be in expanding your business network.

If you give your customers a great experience, they will give you rave reviews and recommend you to their friends. Your concern for their welfare goes much deeper than just providing a great product or service. It involves providing a great experience while you are dealing with them.

The words of Maya Angelou help us to grasp the importance of making sure that our customers feel great while we are interacting with them:

"I've learned that people will forget what you said, people will forget what you did, but people will never forget how you made them feel."

Maya Angelou

You need to be clear about which people you want to make an impact on and what messages you want to convey to them. Once you are clear about your goals, research all the business networking groups where the people you are targeting hang out. You can shortlist a few groups and visit them to see if they are right for you. Several networking groups will allow you to attend a few meetings as a visitor before you sign up to become a member.

Assess the atmosphere at each of the meetings before you make up your mind. Are the leaders adept at managing the group? Do the members have a positive attitude and do they support each other? Are the members of the group from your target audience? If you like what you see, you can compare a few groups before you decide to join.

Be conversational when you visit networking group meetings. If you show that you are genuinely interested in the members of the group, they will respond with warmth. Share information about your business and be willing to discuss issues you are facing in your line of work. Members of the group may suggest innovative solutions to problems you have been facing for a long time.

Once you have joined a few groups, you can attend meetings and make friends with members you like. Volunteer your services, sponsor community projects and be ready to take on leadership positions. This will help you to make a bigger impact and you will be able to grow your business network faster. You can also get tips, advice and referrals from members of the groups.

If you are able to build trust and relationships, you will get a reputation for being a helpful and resourceful person who stands by members of the group. People will come to you for suggestions, advice, referrals, and more. They will invite you to speak at public meetings and those who are making difficult choices or struggling to set up their businesses will seek your advice.

This may seem like a lot of effort without getting anything in return, but it can help you to expand your business network rapidly. Your reputation will grow and it will be much easier for you to grow your business.

To make an impact, you must dress appropriately and look like a successful professional. Most people will form an impression about you quickly based on how you look. You need to wear clothes that fit well and are suitable for the occasion and time of day.

Introduce yourself with a smile and a firm handshake. Be ready to reach out to other people before they approach you. Say hi and pronounce your name clearly when you introduce yourself. Make sure that you have a set of fresh visiting cards at hand. When it's time to part, remember to take the names of the people you met and say how much you enjoyed spending time with them. Say that you would like to meet them again and ask them for their business cards.

Be clear about what you do and who your customers are. You must be able to quickly convey how you are better than your competitors. It is essential to communicate that you are an experienced professional. Create a concise summary that lists all these points and be ready to convey this information quickly and effectively to anyone you meet.

When other members provide referrals, you need to follow up on them promptly. Thank those who have provided referrals and ask them if you can help them in any way. Try to provide referrals to people regardless of whether they have helped you or not. Keep in touch with the members of your groups regularly. Small steps can help you to expand your business network quickly!

These questions will help you to make an impact at meetings:

1. Are you attending the right business networking meetings?
2. Are you helping members of your groups to succeed?
3. Have you prepared an effective elevator pitch?
4. Are you providing referrals to other members of your networking groups?

Chapter 9. How To Engage Effectively

Knowing how to engage effectively with your target audience will help you to expand your business network. It is much easier to engage if you are an extrovert and enjoy chatting with people. However, if you tend to avoid talking too much with strangers, you need to learn the art of making small talk. Casual conversation can help you to engage and build strong relationships.

In an ideal situation, small talk can help you to break the ice and start meaningful conversations. It can help you to get to know the other person and to look for common interests. You can explore ways of helping each other in business and the possible need for your products or services. Informal meetings can also help you to identify your differences and to find out if you enjoy spending time with each other.

The goal is not to find a new customer or to establish a close friendship in the first meeting, though it can and does happen. The aim is to find common interests and reasons to connect with the other person in the future. This is much easier if you are adept at making small talk and know how to get people to relax and open up. Introduce yourself with a smile and a firm handshake to ensure that you will start off on the right foot.

A few open ended questions can get the conversation going. If you listen carefully and respond to what the other person says, it will be easy to keep the conversation flowing without any awkward silences. You can prepare a few questions in advance, which will help you to get you started. If you find that you have a lot in common and are able to connect with the other person, you can spend more time together and take the relationship to the next level.

However, if you find that the other person is not paying attention and doesn't seem to be interested in what you say, it may be best to take that as a signal to move on. A brief initial interaction can help you to decide whether there are reasons to connect with the other person in the future. You can form an impression and decide quickly about whether you like, respect and trust the other person.

The words of John C. Maxwell help us to appreciate the importance of paying attention to verbal and non-verbal communication while interacting with someone:

"People may hear your words, but they feel your attitude."

John C. Maxwell

You can engage with people and develop deeper connections by finding common interests that are not related to your work. Conversations about business may be quite limited apart from asking people what they do and which areas they specialize in. Be open and frank while speaking about yourself. This will in turn encourage others to be forthright while speaking about themselves.

You need to be clear about what you do and how your products or services are better than those offered by your competitors. To expand your business network, you need to be ready to convey that you offer high-quality products or services and to highlight your high level of competence. This is essential if you are to develop your network and get more leads, customers, and orders.

Try to maintain the right balance between personal and business talk. If you talk too much about your business, people may get bored and drift away. You may be giving them more information about your business than they need or want. However, if you don't talk about your work at all, people may assume that you don't do much or that you are not good at what you do. The very purpose of attending a networking event will be defeated and you will not be able to make an impact or to grow your business network.

Avoid monopolizing the conversation and give others a chance to share their ideas and views. Express your opinions assertively while appreciating the point of view of others. If you disagree with someone, try to express yourself without hurting the person. There is no need to think of every conversation as a debate that must be won. Instead of trying to score points over others, try to defuse tension and change the topic.

If you find that the conversation is getting boring, steer it towards topics which interest both of you. This will help to ensure that you will both have a lot to contribute and the meeting will be much more interesting for everyone. You can do some research in advance and think of a few topics that are likely to interest those who will be attending the meeting. Steer the conversation towards the topics whenever there is a pause. Learn to engage effectively to grow your business network quickly!

These questions will help you to engage effectively:

1. Are you adept at making small talk with people you don't know?
2. Have you thought of topics that may interest members of your group?
3. Have you created a brief elevator pitch about what you do?
4. Do you listen attentively and ask questions?

Chapter 10. Be Ready To Face Rejection

You need to be willing to face rejection when you try to expand your business network. You may get a cold response from some people and others may not even be willing to listen to what you are saying. People may disagree with you, criticize you, and oppose you. This is normal and you need to take it in your stride. You control how you react to criticism and whether you will let it upset you.

The words of Bo Bennett help us to realize that rejection is an essential step on the path that leads to success:

"A rejection is nothing more than a necessary step in the pursuit of success."

Bo Bennett

Just as others have the right to react negatively to what you say or do, it is up to you to decide about how you will respond to criticism. You need to be prepared to face rejection and take it as a fact of life over which you have no control. The main thing is to control what you can, which is your response to rejection. There's no need to respond in a negative way. You can choose to respond with grace and humility.

Maintain your internal sense of balance and don't react immediately to rejection. You need to maintain your equanimity regardless of whether you get rejection or praise. Inner balance is a valuable quality that can help you to cope with all sorts of difficult situations.

There is no need to get upset or depressed when you face rejection. Think of it as something that's inevitable when you are striving to achieve great things.

Those who are struggling to deal with their own problems may oppose and criticize you. For example, a person who is facing family or career problems may react negatively to what you say. If you consider this possibility, you will understand the futility of thinking too much about why people are responding negatively to what you say or do. Ruminating over such matters can be a waste of your limited time and energy.

People may be critical of you because of their own insecurities. They may try to put you down to make themselves feel better. It's best to be what you are and let those who reject you deal with their negative views about you. You will not achieve anything by trying to hide your nature and strengths to make them feel comfortable. They may still not accept you and this could prevent you from achieving the great things you know you are capable of.

Be assertive and state what you feel without being aggressive. The more you react negatively to what others are saying, the more they will criticize you. Instead of fretting about what your critics are saying about you, try to focus on all the people who love and respect you. You will find that the vast majority of people are pre-occupied with their own personal issues.

Be prepared to face more and more criticism and opposition when you take on positions of leadership. Some people may not celebrate your successes because they feel threatened by your progress. You need to develop a thick skin to be able to withstand criticism. You may feel that people are treating you unfairly, but always remember that you control how you react.

Choose to focus on the great things you want to achieve in your life instead of thinking about those who you think have rejected you. You need to focus all your energy on achieving your goals as quickly as possible. Stop wasting time thinking about people who criticize and reject you. If they don't approve of you, it's their problem not yours!

As you become successful, more and more people may resent and oppose you. Remember that this has more to do with their insecurity than with your success. Remain positive and focus on your dreams. Look for ways to improve performance and customer satisfaction. Keep providing encouragement, advice and leadership without thinking about what you are getting in return.

Ignore those who reject you and tell you to quit. Listen to your inner voice and stay the course. Remember, negative people cannot offend or upset you unless you allow them to do so. You can choose how you would like to respond to negative comments. Your purpose is to succeed and achieve your dreams, so focus on your goals and tune out the negative voices. Spend more time with positive people who like, support and encourage you!

These questions will help you to find effective ways of coping with rejection:

1. How often do you have to face rejection?
2. Does rejection upset you or do you take it in your stride?
3. Do you realize that all leaders face a lot of opposition?
4. Can you find better ways of dealing with those who reject you?

Chapter 11. Build Trust and Relationships

Building trust and relationships is an essential part of building a powerful business network. A strong network is necessary for success in a complex and uncertain business environment. It can be one of your biggest assets, so invest time in building, expanding and nurturing it. Building a strong network can be a matter of survival for those who are starting out in business. It can help you to get advice, leads, solutions, and referrals when you need them most.

A strong business network that includes people from different fields and locations can support you in different ways. If you only network with people from your own industry, you may not be able to get the type of help you need. A network that includes people from different backgrounds will allow you to access to a wide range of expertise and resources. Members of your network can provide valuable insights and ideas that will help you to solve your problems.

Many entrepreneurs feel that there is no need to build a strong network of friends, advisers, mentors and potential customers. They focus on selling their products or services and think that their business network will develop on its own.

The words of Lindsay Fox help us to appreciate the importance of building relationships and having friends for business success:

"Personal relationships are always the key to good business. You can buy networking; you can't buy friendships."

Lindsay Fox

Reaching out to build relationships comes naturally to some people. Sales professionals do it without thinking. They chat with everyone they meet and are enthusiastic about getting to know people. Their enthusiasm is infectious and people respond positively because they sense genuine warmth and interest.

You need to interact with people without any motive or intention. Showing genuine interest in people from different backgrounds can help you to build a powerful business network. Your attention is the most important gift you can bestow on the other person. Very few people really listen to the things others say as well as what they don't say. Ask people about their families. Ask about what their kids are doing and offer to help them in any way you can. This can make your relationship much stronger.

It is essential to keep in touch with the people you meet. Look for reasons to keep in touch even if you doing business with them. You could forward interesting emails, articles, and jokes. If you share a common interest or hobby, you could inform the other person about events or news related to it. These communications will help to strengthen your relationship and ensure that the person will remain on your network.

Trust is a crucial component of any strong relationship and it takes time to build it. You need to prove to others that you follow through on your commitments. This takes time and those who know you and have worked with you for a while will know if it applies to you or not. You may have developed a trusting relationship with some people over a period of time. With others, you may be just starting out on the journey.

If you are in the initial stages of a relationship, you can build trust quickly by being vulnerable and sharing information about problems that you are facing. Asking others for advice makes them feel important and they are likely to open up to you. Bear in mind that the issues you are discussing need to be appropriate for the stage of the relationship. You can be more open and ask for advice directly once you have developed more trust. You also need to be willing to provide information and advice that the others need.

To build a strong network that can provide the support and advice that you may need in the future, think of the strengths and abilities of each individual. You also need to also be aware of your own strengths. People can offer good advice related to their area of specialization. For example, you could ask different people for technical, legal, financial, marketing or people management advice.

The members of your business network may complement your own strengths and provide just the advice you need to solve problems you are currently facing. You can also provide expert advice to your network on topics about which you have lots of knowledge and experience.

Providing help and advice without considering what you will get in return is essential for success in networking. There is no need to keep assessing what you are getting in return while helping others. Remember, you may get back much more than you are giving in some other form from another person.

Going out of your way to help members will build trust and make the network stronger. While you may also start getting more help in return, bear in mind that people will have higher expectations, which you may or may not be able to meet in the future.

Focus on growing your business network continuously. Be ready to add new members and let go of people who have moved on. This is a natural part of networking, which you need to do continuously.

These questions will help you to find ways to develop trusting relationships with the members of your business network:

1. Do you like to chat with members of your network?

2. Do you discuss your problems with those who can help you?
3. Do you offer help and advice without expecting anything in return?
4. Do you have a network of trusted, loyal advisors?

www.ingramcontent.com/pod-product-compliance
Lightning Source LLC
Chambersburg PA
CBHW052203110526
44591CB00012B/2054